BIG CATS

BIG CATS

BRUCE MITCHELL

Galley Press

CONTENTS

First published in Great Britain in 1979 by
Octopus Books Limited

Published in 1988 by Galley Press, an imprint
of W H Smith Limited.
Registered No 237811 England
Trading as W H Smith Distributors
St John's House
East Street
Leicester
LE1 6NE

ISBN 0 86136 059 1

Printed by Mandarin Offset in Hong Kong

INTRODUCTION

It is generally accepted that there are 37 species of cats in the world today. They range from the domestic tabby that stretches contentedly in front of your fire and which occasionally gives in to its primitive hunting instincts, dropping a half-dead bird at your feet, to the mighty lions of Africa and South Asia which depend on their hunting instincts and skills for survival.

Strictly speaking, only five of these species are 'big cats'. They all belong to the *Panthera* family and with the exception of the jaguar and the cougar which are peculiar to the American continent they are all found in Africa and Asia. The jaguar (*Panthera onca*) lives in the dense forests of America and weighs up to 300 lb (135 kg). Its coat is yellow with black spots arranged in rosettes of four or five around a central spot. The other four 'big cats' are the lion (*Panthera leo*), the tiger (*Panthera tigris*), the snow leopard, or ounce, (*Panthera uncia*), and the leopard (*Panthera pardus*).

However, the term 'big cat' has been applied to nine other species which are not members of the *Panthera* family. These are seven of the larger members of the *Felis* family, one *Neofelis* and one *Acinonyx*. The *Felis* family is represented by the lynx (*Felis lynx*), the bobcat (*Felis rufa*), the caracal (*Felis caracal*), the serval (*Felis serval*), the African golden cat (*Felis aurata*), the Asiatic golden cat (*Felis Temmincki*) and the puma (*Felis concolor*). The other two 'big cats' that we shall look at are the clouded leopard (*Neofelis nebulosa*) and the cheetah (*Acinonyx jubatus*).

One of the common characteristics of all these species is that they are carnivores. They eat the raw flesh of other animals which they stalk, hunt and kill with devastating efficiency. Some of them hunt alone, some hunt in groups. We shall look at this more closely when we discuss the hunting abilities of the big cats in Chapter 3, but obviously to survive as hunters, the cats must have developed special skills and abilities which have enabled them to survive for as long as they have.

Carnivores are descended from the first mammals that appeared 180 million years ago during the Jurassic period of the Mesozoic Era. The first recognizable carnivore was probably the sabre-tooth cat that lived 25 million years ago during the Miocine Epoch of the Cenozoic Era. It has been extinct for many millions of years, but its descendents are still with us.

As flesh-eating hunters, the cats have adapted to their way of life admirably. Their bodies are lean and muscular. Speed is of the essence when going in for the kill and therefore the leg muscles are particularly strong. They have good senses of sight and hearing, although their sense of smell is very often only fair. Because most cats are nocturnal in their habits – with the exception of the cheetah – their sight is particularly sharp. Large eyes enable them to see at night when the amount of light is low.

They all have long, highly sensitive whiskers on their faces. These aid the cats when stalking, enabling them to keep their eyes firmly on their prey, and yet

The cheetah (*Acinonyx jubatus*)

to be aware of any obstacle that may be in their way as they stalk.

All the cats – again with the exception of the cheetah – have retractile claws. The claws are attached to a muscle that enables the cats to draw their claws into sheaths in their paws when walking. Thus their footsteps cannot be heard and the claws are kept sharp. But when they attack, the hook-shaped, needle-sharp claws are extended so that the prey can be pulled down and held firmly. The claws also enable the cats to climb trees.

If you were to look at the paw marks of a big cat, you might assume that there were four toes on each paw. However, there are five toes on each front paw, but as the extra one is raised, it does not register in the traces.

The phrase 'to move like a cat' is well-observed. All cats move with amazing agility and spring with frightening suddenness. Agility is permitted to such a degree because the small clavicle does not connect with other bones but is buried in the muscles of the shoulder region. This allows the cats to spring without the danger of a supporting structure being fractured. Extra force for springing is given by the powerful muscles of the hindlegs and the muscles of the back which the cat uses to straighten the spine when running in pursuit of prey.

Most cats have a short face and a rounded head. The comparatively short face is caused by the fact that cats have relatively few teeth – usually about thirty. The incisors are small and chisel-like, and the canines are long and pointed. The premolars are sharp as is the lower molar which is more elongated. The teeth are used for tearing flesh off a carcass rather than for chewing. The strong muscles of the jaw restrict the amount of lateral movement and so most of the big cat's food is swallowed in chunks which are relatively unchewed. These are broken down by enzymes in the digestive tract, but this can take some time to happen. Thus most of the big cats live on a 'feast and famine' basis. They gorge themselves with the meat of their prey and then fast for some time before eating again.

It is unfortunate that many of the big cats have gained reputations as maneaters. It is true that they are dangerous animals, especially when they are hungry, but in most cases, the maneater is an old cat unable to stalk and to kill its prey.

It is also unfortunate that the skins of many of the big cats are considered attractive when stripped off their dead owners and made into coats which many people consider glamorous. The demand for pelts and the prices that dealers were prepared to pay for them led to many species of big cats being threatened with extinction. Before World War II there were 40,000 tigers in India. Today, the number is reckoned to be around 1,000. Fortunately for future generations, the endangered species are now legally protected: National Parks have been established where cats and other animals can survive, without threat of being hunted by man, in their natural surroundings where they can be seen in all their awe-inspiring beauty.

What are the Big Cats?

We do not know what the first 'life' on earth looked like. Scientists believe that it first appeared around 1,100 million years after the planet was formed 4,600 million years ago. They believe that the first life appeared in the seas of Precambrian times and that by a gradual process of evolution and adaptation all the species that are alive today (at least one and a half million of them) survived and developed. Millions of others have died out since life began and no doubt many of today's animals and plants will no longer be around millions of years from now and new ones will have taken their place. Evolution is a continuous process and did not suddenly stop when man gained supremacy.

Geologists have divided the age of the earth into four distinct eras each of which are split up into periods and in the case of the Tertiary and Quaternary periods are further broken down into epochs. The Precambrian era represented the first age (over 4,000 million years) between the origin of the earth and the first appearance of multicellular organisms. The next era – the Palaeozic – lasted for 345 millions of years and saw the origins of the major plant and animal families. It includes the Devonian period known as the 'Age of Ferns' or the 'Age of Fishes'. The next era, the Mesozoic, is often referred to as the 'Age of Reptiles' and includes the times when the huge dinosaurs roamed the earth. It lasted for 160 million years. During this period the first mammals appeared and in the Cenozoic era – the last 65 million years – the mammals gained supremacy, spread over the planet and evolved into a wide variety of species – including man and the big cats.

Mammals give birth to live young and feed them on milk produced in the mammary glands. It seems strange to consider

Why, you may ask, begin a book on big cats with pictures of a raccoon (**below left**), a mongoose (**left**) and a weasel (**below**)? What do they have in common with big cats? They all belong to the same class, *Mammalia*, and they are all of the order *Carnivora*. That means that they all give birth to live young and meat is an essential part of their diet. All carnivores are descended from the Miacidae family which lived on the earth 65 million years ago during the Eocene period. Then the process of evolution carried on and the carnivores developed different characteristics according to various factors of environment, diet and specialized needs. So despite the obvious physical differences between the animals shown here and the cats we shall be talking about, there are similarities between all members of the same class and order.

that even as the dinosaurs were trundling the earth, the first mammals had already made their appearance. They maintained a low profile ranging in size from that of a mouse to that of a cat and it was not until the dinosaurs died out that the mammals came into their own. They spread all over the world.

The cats are all descended from the family Miacidae which first appeared in North America (as we would call it today). Fossils of cats have been found in rock that is 40 million years old – so had we been around then we may well have been able to recognize some of the animals as cats.

These cats fall into two distinct groups. The first group contained animals such as smilodon – the legendary sabre-toothed cat. They belonged to a family known as Machairodontinae which had developed extended upper canine teeth which resembled sabres. They had lost their lower canines completely. For some reason we have not yet discovered, all the machairodontinae became extinct at around the same time – around 2 million years ago. We do know that today's big cats cannot stand extremely hot temperatures so perhaps there was a general rise in temperatures which caused them to pass away: or perhaps they became prone to some disease which affected them in this drastic way. Whatever the reason, the second groups of cats whose dental structures, cranial formations and hunting instincts are almost identical to today's cats, were left behind to breed and flourish.

All known species of animals were classified in the eighteenth century under a system defined by a Swede called Linnaeus. Families are defined as species which are descended from a common ancestor who lived comparatively recently. Groups of families with a broadly inherited resemblance are classified into orders, which are taken as part of a larger group, a class.

Cats are mammals. This means that they give birth to live young which they feed on their own milk. Man is a mammal, but unlike the cat is not a carnivore. Cats are carnivorous, therefore they are classified as belonging to the order *Carnivora*,

an order which includes the dog family and others.

The family is then broken down into genus and species. Most cats belong to the genus *felis*: the larger ones – leopards, tigers, lions and jaguars – belong to the genus *panthera*.

Thus, cats are related to other carnivores, but not as closely related as they are to each other. The common characteristics they share are the ability to retract their claws (with the exception of the cheetah which is classified separately into the genus *acinonyx*): the hyoid bone which supports the tongue is, in the genus *felis*, completely ossified and partially so in the genus *panthera*. In the smaller cats (*felis*) this partial ossification restricts the movement of the larynx in relation to the skull giving them weak, shrill voices. In the genus *panthera* this permits greater movement of the larynx allowing them their distinctive powerful roar.

The cheetah has the ossified hyoid of the *panthera* but lacks the retractile claws of them and the *felis*. It cannot fit into either genus and is classified in the genus *acinonyx*.

As we said in the introduction, all the cats dealt with in this book live by stealth and their bodies have become adapted over hundreds of thousands of years to the lives they lead. Lean, graceful bodies, powerful leg muscles, specially formed teeth, and coats which merge into their backgrounds enable them to live successful lives as predators – genuinely the supreme hunters of the animal kingdom.

Note the similarity between the red fox (**below left**) (class: *Mammalia*; order: *Carnivora*; family: *Canidae*; genus and species: *Vulpus vulpus*) and the coyote (**below**) (which belongs to the same class, order and family as the red fox, but which is classified *Canas latrans* in its genus and species). All plants and animals were classified by the Swedish biologist Linnaeus in the eighteenth century. Animals with broadly similar ancestry and background are grouped into classes. These are subdivided into order, family, genus and species. Thus, the fox and the coyote are bound to be similar belonging to the same class, order and family. The big cats we shall be discussing are all mammals.

Left: The dental structure of the big cats has become specially adapted to their lives as predators. Some of the teeth are ideally suited for tearing the flesh off their prey, while others are used for breaking the chunks down to smaller pieces.

Below left: It may seem from this illustration that the lion has four toes; in fact the front feet have five, one, corresponding to the human thumb, being set higher than the rest, does not reach the ground and therefore does not make an imprint as the cat walks. On the hind feet shown here, the first toe (which would correspond to the human big toe) is missing completely. The paws are digitigrade which allows the cats to walk on tip toe. This effectively makes the legs longer and adds to the stealth with which the cat can stalk its prey. The claws are retractile which means that they can be drawn back. This is facilitated by a system of muscles and tendons. Because the claws can be drawn back, the claws remain sharp as they are not blunted as the animal moves around often on rocks and hard ground which would wear the claws down rendering them gradually less effective.

Below: Lions are classified class: *Mammalia*; order: *Carnivora*; family: *Felidae*; genus and species: *Panthera leo*. They are the only cats that live in social groups – known as prides. The constitution of the prides varies from group to group but generally there are two males, seven or eight females and a flexible number of cubs. The lionesses are not afraid of the lion, despite his magnificent appearance and, as this picture shows, will strike at them with their claws when trying to fend them off. This would normally happen during the mating season as part of courtship when the female is on heat.

Left: Members of the cat family are adept at climbing trees. The bobcat (*Felis rufa*) is the wildcat of America and is so named because of its short (bobbed) tail and its lolloping gait. It will often take refuge in a tree, especially if it is being hunted by dogs which lack the facility to climb. The scratch marks on the tree indicate that it has been climbed many times before – a sure sign of bobcat country.

Right: Leopards (*Panthera pardus*) are among the most beautiful members of the cat family as well as skilled and accurate hunters. They will often drag their prey into the branches of a tree and eat their fill – returning to the same carcass when they are hungry again. If the prey was left on the ground, scavengers would soon polish off the remains leaving little but the bones. Trees also give the leopard some degree of protection, especially when they are in foliage. The spots blend superbly with the leaves. Older cats often lie in the branches waiting for prey to pass below. One lethally accurate spring gives the prey little chance of escape. Note how well the leopard has positioned its prey on the branch. Here the prey is quite secure, even if the leopard leaves it for any length of time. The expression on the cat's face, accompanied by growling and snarling would frighten off any other predator who wants to share the leopard's meal.

Overleaf: Asleep after gorging itself on its prey, the leopard has balanced itself comfortably and securely in the branches of a tree. Even asleep, the leopard still gives an impression of grace and power. They are usually seen alone – only during mating or while a mother is bringing up her cubs will more than one be seen together. The leopard is at home wherever it can find enough food, water and cover, and this adaptability to a variety of landscapes has assisted the leopard in its fight for survival.

Left: The Asiatic golden cat (*Felis Temmincki*) which is found in south-east Asia and Sumatra is one of the few cats with an evenly coloured brown coat. It has no particular markings except for two black stripes on its cheeks. Like all carnivores it evolved from the Miacidae family. They first appeared in North America 65 million years ago and crossed into Asia by way of the land bridge that used to join the two continents.

Right: Note how brightly the cat's eyes shine. This is caused by the reaction of light on pigmented choroid of the eye which has a tremendous reflective capacity. The layer of cells nearest the retina is made up of fibrous material that reflects the light. The dim night light enters the eye and impinges on the retina. It is reflected from the choroid and this encourages the cells of the retina to catch stronger visual images. The cells of the retina are specially adapted for maximizing the amount of light that enters the eye.

Below: The European wild cat (*Felis sylvestris*) could almost be mistaken for a domestic cat. It is found in northern Europe and the north of Scotland living off the abundant natural resources of the countryside. The wildcat is probably an ancestor of the domestic cat as many experts consider that the first cat to be domesticated was the African bush cat. When it was introduced into Europe the European wild cat was admixtured, resulting millions of years later in today's domestic cat.

Big Cats of the world

The distribution of modern mammals is the subject of some controversy. It seems that during the Cretaceous period (between 65 and 135 million years ago) there were two large continents – Laurasia in the northern hemisphere and Gondwanaland in the southern hemisphere. Part of the southern American portion of Gondwanaland contained early placental mammals. By early Tertiary times Gondwanaland had split into separate South American, African, Indian and Antarctic/Australian parts. At the same time there was a mixture of placental life in Laurasia (North America, Europe and Asia). During the Miocene, Africa and India collided with Laurasia and in the Pleistocene a connection between South and North America was formed. Thus the family Miacidae, the ancestor of all canivores including the cat family, spread from North America, down to South America, across the land bridge that joined America to Asia and into Europe.

If we look at the big cats (by our definition of them) we can see how they are distributed today and how they have adapted to their environment.

The only one which is found in Europe is the lynx, which is also found in North Asia and North America. Its fur varies from a pale dusty grey to rusty red with white on the underparts. Its summer coat is thin and poor, with black spots. This allows it to blend into the background during the summer months when the temperature is warmer. During winter the coat becomes dense and soft and the spots grow paler. The Spanish lynx is shorter with a more heavily spotted coat, whereas in Canada the coat has longer hair and there are hardly any spots.

The jaguar of North, Central and South America has a yellow coat which becomes paler underneath. The body is a mass of black spots, usually four or five arranged around a central spot. On the head and legs, these are more tightly packed. Again this coat offers almost perfect camouflage in the dense forests in which it is usually found.

The other two cats of the American continent are the bobcat and the puma. The colour of the bobcat's coat is influenced by the parts of North America in which it is found. It is usually a

Right: Spot the cat. The puma (*Felis concolor*) is superbly camouflaged. Pumas – also known as cougars or mountain lions – are found from western Canada to Patagonia in the western half of South America. They live in mountains, plains, deserts and forests and their environment will be a factor in the colour of their coats which can vary from yellow to red. When young, pumas have light spots and tail rings which they lose as they mature. They are superb hunters and have been known to track prey for up to 50 miles (80 km). Their length can vary from 4 ft (just over 1 m) to 8 ft (about $2\frac{1}{2}$ m). Weights of up to 260 lb (117 kg) have been recorded.

shade of brown, spotted with grey or white. When the bobcat was being ruthlessly hunted by American farmers, there was a dramatic increase in the numbers of rodents and rabbits which attack the farmers' crops. When the farmers turned their attention to trying to control this menace and the bobcat was left in comparative peace, it quickly re-established itself although it is still hunted either for sport or for their soft fur. In some states of America bounties are offered for each 'cat killed.

Pumas bear some resemblance to a lioness with short close, yellowish fur which can take on a reddish tinge. It lives in the mountains, plains and deserts, and is famous for its remarkable skill and stamina. It has been known to drop 60 ft (18 m) on to the ground and can leap upwards to a height of 15 ft ($4\frac{1}{2}$ m).

Left: The graceful, elegant cheetah (*Acinonyx jubatus*) sits in a typical cat-like position, its feet out in front. They are the only big cats which cannot retract their claws entirely which means that their claws are not as sharp as other big cats. They prefer to live in open country and their legendary speed enables them to catch their prey by sprinting after it. Surprisingly, if a cheetah is caught and trained as a cub it will make an affectionate and playful pet. But beware of being tempted by a vision of taking the cheetah for a walk! Apart from being very expensive to keep, playing with 600 lb (270 kg) of sinewy flesh, with non-retractile claws and a strong hunting instinct could lead to all sorts of dangers.
Top: The tiger is well camouflaged as it rests in the long grass of Kanha, in India. Not that the tiger has a great deal to worry about when it comes to being preyed upon – it is usually the hunter, rarely the hunted. The striped brown coat merges with the background so well that the tigers can approach to within quite close distances of unsuspecting prey before making a lethal spring to bring its prey down.

For some reason, although the common ancestor of the cats began life in North America, these are the only four big cats found there today.

All the others are found in Asia and Africa. Asia boasts the caracal (desert lynx), the Asiatic golden cat (Temminck's cat), the leopard, clouded leopard, snow leopard, tiger and the cheetah. Africa has the caracal, serval, African golden cat, lion, leopard and cheetah.

Generally, the species of big cats with spotted coats are found in the forest regions. Thus the leopard, which lives in deep tropical forests of Asia and Africa as well as in bush country, merges into its background as the colour and length of the coat vary with locality and climate. Usually the ground colour is tawny yellow with white underparts. The black spots are arranged in rosettes. The clouded leopard of south Asia has large, dark grey spots on a yellowish coat, which allows it to move around in the shadows of the forest almost unnoticed.

The tiger has superb protective colouring. It is brownish with large black stripes. It moves around the jungle in the twilight, almost invisible, blending so beautifully with its background, that it can creep, almost completely unnoticed, to within springing distance of its unsuspecting prey.

The lion has no need of spots or stripes. It lives in the dry, brown savannah land of Africa which its coat matches perfectly.

The caracal is tawny on the flanks and lightly spotted on the underside, and the African golden cat is aptly named being short haired and golden brown with a white underside. It lives in the equatorial forests of Africa feeding on rodents and birds.

Another cat with a more or less uniformly coloured coat is Temminck's cat which has no particular markings apart from two black stripes on its cheeks. It is found in south-east Asia and Sumatra – thousands of miles away from the birthplace of its prehistoric ancestor.

23

Left: The increasingly rare snow leopard (*Panthera uncia*) lives in mountainous areas of Asia, around the Himalayas and the Altais. It can live in altitudes of up to 19,000 ft (6,000 m) and only descend to 6,000 ft (2,000 m) in winter. It is the supreme mountain cat, its thick coat giving it protection against the cold of a Himalayan winter. Its pelt was in such demand by furriers that it has almost been hunted out of existence – although it represented no threat to man, his crops or his livestock because of the inaccessible areas in which it lives. It preys upon wild mountain goats and small mammals, its method of attack being the same as that of most other cats – stealth and spring.

Below left: The black panther (*Panthera pardus*) is the same genus and species as the leopard. They occur sporadically, but are more common in south Asia than anywhere else in the leopards' domain. Note the strong fang-like teeth ideal for tearing at prey. Like all leopards, the black panther can develop strong food preferences and may travel long distances from its day bed to its hunting ground, without disturbing likely prey on the way. They may hunt during the day, but if they live in an area where they are hunted, they will hunt at night. Obviously, the colour of their coats offers superb protection in darkness. Then all that would be visible would be the light shining in their eyes. The panther may look extremely fierce, but like most big cats it will not attack man unless threatened or unable to hunt naturally.

Right: The lynx is widespread across Canada (*Lynx canadensis*), Scandinavia, the USSR and Asia (*Lynx lynx*) and in Spain and the Balkans (*Lynx pardellus*). It can grow up to $3\frac{1}{2}$ ft (1 m) long and weigh up to 40 lb (18 kg). The lynx lives in forests which they seldom leave. They hunt at night, always alone. Their keen sight has given rise to the expression 'as sharp eyed as a lynx' and they will trail prey for long distances. Their diet includes hares, rabbits, grouse and small deer. Like many other big cats the lynx has suffered from over-hunting by man who values the fur of their coats.

Left: *Felis Temminicki* – the Asian golden cat – is the typical wild cat of the equatorial forests of Asia. It is the only cat that penetrates the thick undergrowth. More heavily built and larger than the serval cat, the golden cat is a shy creature and difficult to catch sight of because of the stealth with which it moves around the jungle. It hunts rodents and birds – usually at twilight or night.

Below left: The rarest of all the big cats is the clouded leopard, found in the regions south of the Himalayas across into Indonesia. Like other leopards, the clouded variety spends much of its time in trees – where it catches birds with tremendous agility. It can measure up to 1½ ft (40 cm) at the shoulders and its total length including the tail can extend to over 6 ft (2 m). It is called 'clouded' because of the pattern on its coat, which was highly prized because of its rarity value. It is classified alone among the genus *Neofelis* as it shares an identical cranial and dental structure with the genus *Panthera* and a number of other features with the genus *Felis*. Many zoologists, therefore, regard the clouded leopard as a link between the two genera.

Below: The serval (*Felis serval*) or African leopard cat is found in the open savannah or sometimes where the vegetation is much denser. There are two varieties of the species – first, the true serval cat which has a series of dark stripes on a brownish background merging over the flanks into a series of well-marked spots, and, second, the servalena which is only found in the western regions of Africa in the humid, well-wooded savannah. It used to be considered a distinct species, but it is now accepted that the differences are so minimal that this separate classification is no longer justified.

Above: The panther (black leopard) is one of the many species of leopard. This one was photographed in Randolph Park Zoo in Tuscan, U.S. one of the many zoos established around the world where we can see animals that most of us would never see alive. Zoos also allow biologists to study the animals at closer quarters than would otherwise be possible, thus increasing our store of knowledge of the big cats.

Right: The leopard is found in parts of Asia and over much of Africa. There may be as many as seventeen different varieties of the species *Panthera pardus* which vary in size and colouring. Although they are often found in savannah lands, they also occur in the mountainous regions of Africa and Asia and in a few forested areas. They have acquired an unjustified reputation as maneaters which may have arisen out of the leopard's tendency to develop a taste for a particular type of meat. Human flesh being no exception, if a leopard does happen to kill and eat a man, it may be satisfied with little else from then on.

Right: At one time the cheetah was widely dispersed from India, across to the north of Africa, down that continent into South Africa. Today, it is mainly found in Africa and is probably extinct in other parts of the world. It prefers to live in open country – one of the reasons for its decline in Asia. As agriculture spread, the cheetah's natural habitat was threatened as its diet of blackback and axis deer disappeared. Cheetahs live solitary lives, but occasionally they hunt in pairs and there have been reports of groups of up to twelve hunting and living together. Such groups would be composed of males and females or exclusively male – never all female! The natural prey of the cheetah is Thompson's and Grant's gazelle, zebra and occasionally birds, such as bustards and guinea fowl.

The bobcat (**below**) (*Felis rufa*) is the wild cat of the American continent. It can weigh up to 20 lb (9 kg) and extend to just over 3 ft (1 m) in length. Its ears are tipped with pointed tufts of hair which are said to increase the hearing capacity of the animal. The territorial area that the bobcat covers will vary in size according to the quantity of food available. One cat has been known to cover a tract of land 50 miles (80 km) in diameter. But if there is an abundance of food – rabbits, deermice, wood rats and squirrels, which make up the bulk of the bobcat's diet – the cat may confine itself to an area of 5 miles (8 km) in diameter, or even less. They stalk their prey and kill it by jumping on its back, tearing at the neck until the prey is dead. The bobcat, itself, is part of the diet of the puma and large foxes; owls will attack and kill bobcat kittens which are fiercely defended by the mother cat. The 'cat has proved itself to be very adaptable, changing its habits to accommodate the replacement of its natural habitat by towns and cities. It is however a solitary animal, the only contact it has with other 'cats is during the mating season and the only social unit of which it is ever a part is when it is dependent on its mother, or when rearing her own young.

The jaguar (**left and below**) is the largest of the American cats. It lives mainly in the dense forests of Central and South America, although some are found in the plains of Patagonia and the mountain ranges of the Andes. They are agile tree climbers and extremely good swimmers. Fish forms part of their diet, being caught with a deft flick of the paw, flipping it out of the water. Jaguars are enormously intelligent and stories of them using their tails as lures to attract fish may be true. Like many cats, the jaguars appear to have their own territory which they will defend against intruders, but because they are solitary animals and difficult to spot because of their superb camouflage, much of our knowledge is sketchy and based on reports, stories and legends of South American Indians.

The best hunters

The big cats are the supreme hunters! Of all the animals in the world, cats have perfected their hunting techniques down to the finest of fine arts. To watch a domestic cat slink through a garden in pursuit of a bird or a rat will give you some idea of the elegance and grace with which larger cats move, and the stealth with which they stalk.

Their hunting is not only of importance to the cats themselves – it also plays an important part in maintaining the ecological balance of an area. The weaker and older members of a herd of antelope or zebra are easier for a big cat to stalk and spring on. Thus the big cats play a part in ensuring that only the strongest members of a species on which they prey have a good chance of survival and therefore of reproduction.

It is therefore of some concern that many of the big cats are in danger of extinction – not only because the world would be a poorer place without these creatures of extreme grace and beauty, but also, it is the law of nature that a delicate balance must be maintained between hunter and hunted, and if this balance is shifted, the results can be disastrous.

In the Western United States, the puma and the lynx were ruthlessly hunted by man because of the damage they caused,to flocks of sheep and herds of cattle. As the population of big cats declined, there was a sharp increase in the number of rodents upon which they preyed. As rodents can cause tremendous damage to crops and poultry, the farmers set about destroying them. The cats were left in comparative peace to re-establish themselves, but finding that their natural diet had been vastly reduced, they began to attack sheep and cattle with even more frequency than before.

Wild herbivores, such as deer, are the prey of the Indian lion. Left to breed and procreate, a herd of deer can quickly strip an area of foliage. While the Indian lion was common, a balance was maintained, but now that they are so scarce, the ungulates are left unchecked to strip an area of new saplings thus preventing the continuing growth of forested places which offer protection to a wide variety of animal life.

Much the same happened in Africa. Because the wild

Left: A cheetah after a successful kill. The prey is a Thomson's gazelle. Many other big cats lie in wait and set ambushes for their prey – not the cheetah. It relies on its speed to capture the animals it preys upon, being able to run at up to 50 mph (80 km/h). It stalks the animal, choosing one that has become separated from a group and then sprints after it. If the prey has a good start, the cheetah may well give up the chase as it can only keep up top speed for a short time. But if the prey is within striking distance the cheetah will spring at it or overtake it and trip it up with its front paws. Once on the ground, the animal has no chance of escape. The cheetah dispatches prey by biting into its jugular vein and death follows quickly.

antelope was in some danger, many of its predators were ruthlessly put down. The deer herds grew to such an extent that much of the vegetation in the area was destroyed as the competition for food increased within and amongst the herds.

And so it is that natural hunters should be left to hunt naturally, and the big cats are among the most efficient hunters in the animal kingdom. They are masters at stalking their prey – creeping up to within a few yards of it – and springing forward to bring it to the ground. Once on the ground the prey has little chance of escape. The curved claws of the cats tear at the throat and neck and the victim is soon dead. Some of the cats, particularly the leopard and the jaguar and mountain lion will spring on unsuspecting creatures from the branches of a tree, and the tiger, if it is hungry, will leap from the undergrowth to pounce on an animal that is passing its lair.

Stealth is essential, because although the big cats can run at speeds of up to 40 mph (64 km/h) they are unable to keep up these speeds for any great distances. A fleet footed prey stands a reasonable chance of escape if the initial spring of the cat is unsuccessful in bringing it to the ground. The cheetah does often catch its prey in flight and is said to use a unique method of bringing down its prey. Cheetahs are capable of speeds of up to 70 mph (110 km/h) and can sustain this for a longer period than other big cats at top speed. Recent films have shown that the cheetah as well as springing to bring down its prey, often overtakes it and trips it up with its paws. Once on the ground the prey – gazelle or impala – stands no chance. But if the animal escapes and there is nothing else in sight, the cheetah will content itself with a much smaller meal, such as a hare.

Most cats hunt at night. Their eyes are specially designed for the purpose, containing a substance called guanin that lines the surface of the cats' eyes. The effect of this can be seen in the eyes of an ordinary domestic cat. If a light is shone into a cat's eyes, you can probably detect a coppery-green glare. This is due to the reflection of guanin. It intensifies any light that enters a cat's eyes and, as the muscles of the eye widen at night to increase the amount of light that enters, the cat's ability to see at night is increased.

Again the exception is the cheetah. Although it hunts in the twilight, it also hunts in the early morning. Like most of the other cats, the cheetah will stalk a herd and select its victim, usually one that has become separated from the other animals. It then gives chase, and more often than not, brings the prey down.

Above: A bobcat chases a snowshoe rabbit across the snows of North America. The rabbit stands little chance of escape – one spring from the 'cat will bring it down on the rabbit's back, giving the 'cat enough food to survive for another day.

The big cats are also helped in their search for prey by the superb camouflage that their colourings and markings give them. The stripes of the tiger merge with the long grass in which they hunt. The spots and rosettes of other cats make them almost indiscernible from their backgrounds.

Cats are also masters of ambush, especially the leopard. They are marvellous tree climbers and will hide in the protective branches of a tree until their unsuspecting prey passes by. They seize the prey by the neck and kill it by fracturing the neck. Rather than eat on the spot, the leopard will drag its prey to a secluded spot and then gorge itself. If it is unable to finish its meal, it will haul the carcass up into a tree well away from scavenging hyenas and jackals.

The diet of the big cats varies from area to area. Deer, antelope, gazelles, warthogs, even arboreal monkeys and birds are not safe from the cats. Most small ungulates are hunted with the ruthless efficiency that marks these animals as the supreme hunters of the animal kingdom.

Below: It is almost impossible to estimate the actual speed of a cheetah running at full stretch. It can only keep this up for short distances after which it soon tires. One estimate put the maximum speed at over 70 mph (112 km/h) and acceleration at 45 mph (72 km/h) after two seconds. Because of the way the backbone is formed, the cheetah is able to gather itself together and extend itself to full stretch, thus increasing the length of its pace and giving the beast superb springing powers as well. Because the night vision of the cheetah is not so effective as it is in other cats, it hunts in twilight or in early morning. It often attacks animals that have become separated from the rest of their herd or older and more infirm ungulates, but it fights a running battle with the lion who may try to steal the cheetah's prey after a successful kill.

Below: To spring or not to spring! The bobcat looks at the deermouse – part of its staple diet – as if trying to make up its mind whether or not to pounce.

Left: The bobcat is partial to the taste of fish which it catches with its paw. It may lie on a stone waiting for a likely meal to come by, or it may lie in the water.

Below: The puma eats its fill after a successful deer hunt, shearing off chunks of meat with its carnassial teeth. The development of these teeth is one of the many ways in which the cats have adapted to their carnivorous feeding habits. The three triangular cusps enable the cat to cut through the toughest flesh. The puma is reputed to make a fallen deer last for one week, feeding off it as and when it is hungry and hiding the carcass and returning to it until the flesh has been completely devoured. The puma lives from Western Canada down to Patagonia in South America. They are superb hunters and have been known to track prey for up to 50 miles (80 kilometres).

Right: The bobcat normally stays hidden during the day in a lair between rocks or in caves which are usually carefully lined with dry leaves. It hunts at night but the sight of the plump rabbit which this bobcat has in its mouth must have been tempting enough for the cat to leave its lair and pounce. Farmers would be pleased if the bobcat restricted itself to a diet of jackrabbits and other small creatures which can do damage to their crops, but the 'cat will attack farm livestock and thus incurs the fatal wrath of many an American farmer.

Left: The golden cat is, like all cats, a skilled hunter but it is difficult to determine its dietary habits as it is a shy creature and will slink off – well camouflaged – into the undergrowth at the approach of an animal larger than itself. We know that it eats rodents and birds because of the remains that have been discovered in places where there is evidence of a golden cat's presence.

Below: The cougar or puma, seen here tracking its prey across the snowy wastelands of Colorado in the United States, hunts deer and other mammals, ripping the victim's throat open and drinking the warm blood. The colour of its environment will influence the colour of the puma's coat which can range from yellow to deep red.

Below: The Caracal, which is related to the European and American lynx, is found in East Africa and parts of Asia. It feeds at night on small antelope, rodents and birds and has been known to attack domestic fowl and lambs. Its tail is comparatively short and its long hind legs give it good springing power enabling it, like all big cats, to surprise prey with a sudden leap.

Tigers

Tigers are among the most magnificent of all animals. A large male averages 9 ft (3 m) in length (including its tail). It stands 3 ft (1 m) or more at the shoulder and can weigh up to 500 lb (225 kg). Females are slightly smaller – about 1 ft shorter and 100 lb (45 kg) less in weight.

The colouring of the tiger's coat ranges from fawn to red, and is overlaid with blackish-brown transverse stripes, providing excellent camouflage in forest regions.

Until the nineteenth century, the tiger was widespread from Turkey to China, but it is now in danger of extinction. It is found in parts of India, south-west Asia, Iran, Manchuria, Sumatra, Bali and Java. The total number of tigers living naturally in these areas is now only a few thousand.

The tiger was ruthlessly hunted for sport by wealthy hunters, and, out of fear, by natives. Also, as civilization spread to areas where tigers occurred, vast areas of forest were cleared – robbing the tiger of his natural habitat.

As a result, in 1972, the World Wildlife Fund launched a campaign to protect the tiger. Some countries, including the Soviet Union and India, have banned the hunting of tigers and the export of tiger skins. In the West, the United Kingdom and the United States have put an embargo on the import of the skins.

Like most cats, tigers usually hunt at night. With their superb camouflage they can stalk their prey to within a few yards and then make a surprise attack. They normally fell their prey with one huge leap and bite its neck or throat to kill it. Rather than eat on the spot, the tiger will then drag away the fallen prey to a quiet spot to enjoy its meal. It may then hide the remains of its victim and return to feed again from the same carcass. Deer, antelope and buffalo are the tiger's normal diet, although it also has a weakness for porcupine.

These big cats are solitary creatures. They have their own territory which they will defend furiously. They mark the boundaries with their own urine, the scent of which announces to encroaching tigers that they are trespassing on another's territory. The only contact that one tiger will have with another is when they are mating.

Right: The stealth and grace of the tiger is perfectly captured in this photograph of a wild Bengal tiger. Stealth is vital in stalking prey – antelope, wild pigs, monkeys and, occasionally, porcupines. It stalks for the first part of the hunt and then springs on the prey's back, pinning it to the ground with one paw and tearing at its throat with the other, often breaking its neck in the process by pressing upwards. The Bengal tiger has a short coat with a uniform orange colour, covered with prominent transverse stripes.

Below: Like all cats, tigers spend a great deal of time grooming themselves. Their tongues are rough and this enables them to remove loose fur and insects that have become caught up in their coats. The one thing that grooming will not get rid of is porcupine quills that have become inserted in their paws. As the tiger walks on the afflicted paw, the quill becomes more deeply immersed. In such circumstances the tiger may turn to attacking domestic cattle or even humans. Then its days are numbered for despite bans on tiger hunting threatened villagers will stop at nothing to trap and kill a maneater.

Bottom: Even in the national parks, such as this one in Dudwa in India, the tigers have their own territory. They mark the boundaries by urinating on trees and shrubs all over their areas warning off would-be intruders. This female is sniffing a tree which has been recently marked in this way by an adult male.

Below right: With ears flattened and mouth snarling this superb beast warns a prospective intruder to come no farther. We can clearly see from this illustration how well the tiger's teeth have become adapted for its carnivorous way of life.

The urine of the female tiger has a special smell during oestrus and this acts as a signal to neighbouring males. As soon as courtship has been completed, the male leaves. If he does stay with the female until birth, the female will watch him suspiciously guarding her cubs carefully in case the tiger should try to eat them.

A tiger will not normally attack humans, unless it has been injured and is unable to hunt. One cause of injury is brought about by the tiger's liking for porcupine meat. If the tiger's limbs or paws are pierced by a porcupine quill, it is unable to hunt naturally. As the quill works its way into the tiger's skin, the more acute the pain becomes. In this case the cat may turn maneater (or cattle eater) and then every villager in the area will join in the hunt for the tiger, even in areas where it is protected by law.

There are eight sub-species of tiger. These are the Bengal (*Panthera tigris tigris*), the Indo-Chinese (*Panthera tigris corbetti*), the Balinese (*Panthera tigris balica*), the Javanese

(*Panthera tigris sondaica*), the Caspian (*Panthera tigris virgata*), the Siberian (*Panthera tigris altaica*), the Chinese (*Panthera tigris amoyensis*) and the Sumatran (*Panthera tigris sondaica*).

The Bengal tiger is the instantly recognizable species with its uniform orange coat, white paws and lower parts and dark transverse stripes. The Indo-Chinese is smaller and its coat is slightly darker. It also has more stripes which are shorter and narrower. The Balinese, Javanese and Sumatran tigers are very similar in appearance. They are relatively small and the stripes are less well defined than they are in other varieties. The Sumatran has the darkest fur of all tigers and the Balinese has a very short, lustrous coat. All three varieties are becoming increasingly rare – indeed, there are probably less than ten Javanese tigers alive today and the Balinese may be extinct.

The Caspian tiger has the longest fur of all tigers, and its coat is comparatively dark. The Siberian tiger also has long fur as it has to survive in a bitterly cold climate.

The Chinese tiger is smaller than the Siberian and its coat, although similar in colour to the Bengal tiger is thicker and the stripes are less prominent.

As we said before it is only in the mating season that male and female come together. The actual act of coupling lasts only about twenty seconds, but is repeated several times a day during oestrus. The gestation period is 105 days and normally about three or four cubs are born in each litter. Infant mortality is high and perhaps only around two cubs will survive to adulthood. The cubs are born blind and weigh only about 2 or 3 lb (about $1\frac{1}{2}$ kg). They are born with the tiger's distinctive stripes and grow very rapidly. Their eyes open at fourteen days and they are weaned at six weeks. They can kill for themselves at seven months, but normally they stay with their mother until they are two years old. During this time she teaches the cubs how to hunt so that by the time they are ready to leave and establish their own territory they are well able to fend for themselves. At three years, they are fully grown.

Right: The Siberian tiger (*Panthera tigris altaica*) is longer than its Bengal cousin; it also has a longer, thicker coat which enables it to withstand the intense cold of a Siberian winter. They were once evenly distributed throughout eastern Russia, northern China and northern Korea, but it is estimated that there are only about 200 of them living wild in the world today. The colouring is lighter than other tigers, one of the ways in which it has adapted itself over the centuries to its environment. There are records of pure white tigers, but these are probably genetic freaks rather than a recurring sub-species.

Left: Two Bengal tigers splash about in a stream, obviously enjoying themselves. As we have said, tigers enjoy the cooling effect of water as they cannot stand extreme heat. They have been a threatened species for some time now and we cannot tell what effect the military actions in Vietnam have had on their numbers. Much of the tigers' natural habitat was destroyed by napalm bombing and forest fire.

Left: The Bengal tiger is a strong swimmer and fond of a quick dip. This one was photographed in Singapore and is clearly enjoying the water. The tiger cannot stand excessive heat and will often sit in shallow water in order to keep cool. They are fond of fish as a part of their diet, so water obviously plays an important part in their lives.

Right: The white tiger is not a separate species and is extremely rare. The white coat is due to incomplete albinism and is the result of both parents carrying recessive genes, although they (the parents) are probably normally coloured. White tigers are not nearly so well camouflaged as they stand out much more clearly against their background, and may therefore have a more difficult time in following prey.

Left: This photograph of the tiger quite clearly shows the facial markings that are typical of all their breed. The whiskers are not purely decorative – they are highly sensitive and invaluable to the tiger when stalking prey as they indicate the presence of an obstacle, allowing the tiger to keep its eyes fixed on its intended prey. The angry expression does not indicate a continually fierce animal. There are many reports of human beings passing within close range of a tiger without being threatened. But, like all wild animals, the tiger is extremely dangerous when threatened or when its patience is exhausted.

Left: Claws play an important part in the tiger's struggle for survival. They are essential in killing prey and have to be kept sharp. Most tigers, indeed most cats, sharpen their claws by scratching them against a favourite tree to which they return again and again. This one was photographed in Chitwan National Park in Nepal one of the many areas where hunting by humans is strictly forbidden in an attempt to protect the endangered species of the area.

Top right: Being creatures of habit, tigers will probably use the same watering hole time and time again. They lap water in the same way as a domestic cat using the tongue to take the water into the mouth.

Right: The stripes of the tiger merge beautifully with the leafy jungle background, giving almost perfect camouflage. With their special ability to see at night, tigers are nocturnal creatures and photographs of them in their natural environment are not particularly easy to take. In 1972 the World Wildlife Fund under the presidency of Prince Bernhardt of the Netherlands launched a campaign to save the tiger from extinction and this has met with considerable success.

Lions-the only social cats

Thousands of years ago, lions were common throughout southern Europe, southern Asia, eastern and central India and over the whole African continent. Today, with the exception of a few, highly protected animals in the Forest of Gir in India, the only naturally-occurring lions are found in Africa. But even in Africa, lions have been wiped out in the north.

Perhaps the most famous of all the big cats, lions can vary considerably in size and appearance. A large male can grow up to 10 ft (3 m) in length from nose to the tip of its tail. It may weigh up to 500 lb (225 kg) and stand about 3½ ft (1 m) high at the shoulders. The female is usually smaller. Their coats are short and the colour can range from pale yellow to dark brown. (Recently, white lions have been discovered, but these are probably genetic freaks.)

Most people associate the lion with the large, shaggy mane of the male. This can vary from individual to individual. In some cases, it is entirely lacking, in others it may simply fringe the face and in others it can cover the back of the head, the neck and the shoulders. A fully-maned male lion is a magnificent beast and it is little wonder that he is sometimes called the king of beasts.

Unlike the other big cats in appearance, lions are also unique in their social behaviour. They are gregarious and spend most of their lives in the company of other lions. This group is known as a pride and within it a complicated system of social, hierarchical and reproductive relationships is displayed. Most prides normally include two males who defend the group and the territory in which they live against males from other prides. The pride's territory can extend up to 20 sq. miles (49 sq. km) and to warn off intruders the male lions will urinate on the ground and bushes that border the pride's territory. The pungent smell of the urine lingers on the vegetation warning any intruding beast that he is trespassing.

The females are responsible for finding food. They normally hunt at night preying upon gnus, antelopes, zebras, gazelles and giraffes. They will also scavenge – eating any dead animal they come upon, if they are hungry. Often the male will scare

Left: Two black-maned lions greet each other. The cat family has a complex system of communication within each species. By lowering or raising the voice, or increasing or reducing the rate of purring, the lions can communicate affection, fear, excitement and danger. The ear flaps play an important part in communication. When the beast is calm, the flaps are usually flattened and held slightly to the back of the head. Alertness is indicated by the ears being raised and held taut with the inner surfaces facing forward. The two males shown here belong to the same pride, within which there will be a definitely established social hierarchy. It is probable that the seated lion is superior to the lion that is nuzzling.

prey into an ambush laid by the females. When the lion has separated the intended victim from the rest of a herd it stalks it intently. Because the lion lives in comparatively open country, it must stalk at some distance from its victim. It creeps on its belly, hiding behind low bushes and other natural obstacles that do not look as if they could give any cover at all to the preying lions. When it is within about a hundred yards from the intended prey the stalking lion bursts into a dash and springs upon the victim. In its final charge the lion can reach speeds of up to 40 mph (60 km/h) but it cannot sustain these speeds for any length of time. Thus, if the spring does not succeed or if the prey has become aware that it is being stalked, the antelope, zebra or whatever stands a fair chance of escaping. But if the lion gets its claws into the prey, the struggle is short and bloody. The lion holds the prey firmly by the rump and its great claws tear at its throat.

This plays an important part in the ecological balance of an area. Obviously, the stronger and faster ungulates stand a better chance of escaping from the stalking lion. Older and enfeebled beasts are more liable to fall victim, and therefore the predatory lion helps to maintain a healthy population of ungulates by killing off the weaker beasts. If only the strong survive, only the strong can breed!

Obviously, each pride differs in size and formation. A typical pride consists of two males, seven females and a variable number of cubs. In the Serengeti in west Africa a pride with eleven females has been recorded, the smallest with only two. One pride with six males has been noted.

Lionesses usually come into oestrus at periods of two and a half months throughout the year, but normally they become pregnant in spring or autumn. Gestation is up to 115 days and once the cubs (normally three or four in each litter) are born, the female spends her time taking care of them. It is usual for the lioness to leave the pride and take refuge in a thicket for the actual birth. She may be accompanied by another female who helps in hunting for a few days.

When the cubs are born they are quite helpless and the mother will only leave them to find food. She moves them around every two or three days, carrying them by the mouth, to prevent the den acquiring a smell that might attract predators such as leopards or hyenas who would kill any defenceless cubs they may come across. If this does happen and the mother returns to find some of her cubs dead, she will have no qualms in eating the remains herself.

By the time they are about a month and a half old, the cubs are introduced to the pride. Their fur is longer than that of an adult and their feet look a little too large for their bodies which have traces of spots on them, especially on the forehead.

It is quite likely that another lioness has given birth at the same time and when the cubs of both litters are introduced to the pride, it is not unusual for the cubs to suckle from a lioness who is not their mother. This communal suckling can result in squabbling for nipples. Lion cubs do not establish ownership of a particular nipple but look for any one and try to push off a cub already suckling there. The cub in possession resists, making a high-pitched snarl and tries to swat the would-be usurper.

The advantages of communal feeding are that milk supply is evened out to all the cubs in a pride, and, if a lioness dies or her milk flow ceases, the cubs will not necessarily die.

Right: Lions spend quite a lot of time sitting around and yawning, especially after they have eaten. We can see from this photograph just how well suited the lion's teeth are for the life it leads. Some of them are used for tearing meat off the carcass of dead prey and others for breaking it into smaller pieces. The fully-toothed lion has thirty teeth – twelve incisors (six top and six bottom), four canines (two top and two bottom), six premolars at the top and four at the bottom, and two molars top, two bottom.

Above: All females of the genus *Panthera* squat quietly as the males mount them. During the sexual act the female makes low, pitched growling noises as the male grips her by the scruff of the neck with his teeth. It seems that he does this in such a way that the female feels no discomfort, and some experts consider that the bite is the equivalent of a maternal embrace. The period of gestation for the lioness is between 105 and 113 days and usually three or four cubs will be born. They can begin to breed at the age of two but do not reach their prime until they are about five. All the big cats are induced ovulators – the release of the female ovary is brought about by the act of mating, rather than in a regular cycle as in humans.

Right: Courtship between a lion and a lioness is a spitting, hitting, roaring contest. The lioness indicates that she is in oestrus by a special scent in the urine which is caused by glandular action. The male will follow the female around constantly caressing her. She often responds by spitting and cuffing him. When she is ready to submit she will crouch down indicating to the male that he may mount her. However, it is by no means certain that a female 'in heat' will give in to any of the males in the pride; and a male lion who is frustrated in his amorous advances is a very dangerous beast. The female in this picture has indicated her submission by squatting in the mating position.

Right: There's no need to ask what this young cub has been doing! It has obviously been gorging itself on the carcass of the pride's prey. The cubs are taught how to hunt by means of simulated attacks in the form of games which they play with the adults and between themselves. These games encourage the natural predatory instinct of the youngsters who will be taken on their first hunt quite early on. The lions hunt at night, the male lions often chasing the prey towards a place where the females lie in ambush. As time goes on the young are taught all the wiles of the pride until they are able to make their own way. The young cubs will eat in accordance with the mother's place in the social hierarchy of the pride until it establishes its own place within that hierarchy.

Above: Lions will not normally climb trees, but lionesses may jump on to the low branches to sun themselves in a tree that is within its territory. It has been estimated that the lions spend about four hours out of every day hunting, grooming or in some other activity, and the remaining twenty hours lazing around, sleeping and resting. However, although they may give the appearance of restful calm, the lion is constantly on the alert and will be ready to attack at the least sign of danger.

Left: The sandy colour of the lion's coat is almost the same as the rock on which it sits. The young cub on the right probably joined the pride when it was about ten weeks old and its coat is probably light, two-toned brown which will gradually darken as time goes by. The adult males play a small part in training them for the hunt but when the cubs are about eighteen months old the attitude of the male lion changes. Young males will be forced to leave the pride and young females will have been trained to look after themselves, within the hierarchy of the pride.

Lions are the only gregarious cats, living in prides which can vary in number and constitution. There will usually be at least two adult males, whose role is to defend the pride's territory against the males of other prides: several females who are responsible for hunting prey (often with the assistance of the males) and a variable number of cubs. Within the pride there is a defined social hierarchy which is evident when feeding. The males will eat first, the females second and the cubs last of all. The competition for food can be intense and those unable to hold their place will soon be in danger.

Above left: This magnificently maned lion is aptly called the king of beasts and as such he has no natural enemies apart from man. There may be territorial disputes with other males but often these do not result in a fight. The lion in possession will take up an aggressive posture which may be enough to frighten off the intruder. But accidents can, of course, happen. It has been known for young, inexperienced lions to become impaled on the horns of a sable antelope, or to be trampled by a herd of buffalo.

Above: The female lies in a typical cat position, hind legs tucked in, front ones stretched out in front. Although smaller than the male, the lioness is still a formidable sight. In full flight, they can run at speeds of up to 40 mph (64 km/h), but only in short bursts. They can make standing jumps of 12 ft high (4 m) and leaps of up to 40 ft (12 m).

Left: Two lionesses relax in the grass of the African savannah where the temperature is usually above 64°F (18°C). Heat and dryness are normal throughout the year except in the summer when the heavy rains and lower temperatures make the grasses grow rapidly. This supports a vast amount of wildlife including the ungulates on which the big cats prey. One estimate has put the number of beasts necessary to sustain four lions at one thousand, so the two in this picture would require around 500 every year. Many of the beasts killed will be the old and infirm of the herds; therefore the lions play a part in maintaining healthy wildlife.

Big Cats and their young

With the exception of lions who live a gregarious life within their prides, the main reason for social interaction between cats is breeding. The female indicates that she is in heat by urinating throughout her territory – her urine at the time giving off a peciliar smell which tells to the male that she is ready to mate.

Unlike humans, cats are induced ovulators. Human females become pregnant when a male sperm comes into contact with a female ovum, released in monthly cycles in mature females. This release occurs spontaneously whether or not sexual intercourse is going to take place. In cats, however, the ovum is released by a series of reflexes after mating.

During heat – or oestrus – the ovarian follicles come into maturity and the female is prepared for mating. The ovaries are stimulated by the action of the pituitary gland, situated at the base of the brain. This controls the release of various secretions into the cat's blood stream which bring about ovulation and which find their way into the cat's urine, giving it the peculiar smell which attracts the male.

Once the male has come into contact with the female a courtship ritual is followed which to the human eye may look like the preliminaries to a particularly acrimonious divorce, rather than the act of procreation. A spitting, scratching, cuffing and snarling display is followed by the female squatting calmly while the male mounts her. This is repeated many times as a female who mates regularly throughout oestrus is more likely to ensure that the reflex mechanisms necessary to produce ovulation are triggered off. Strangely enough it has been noted that lions who mate more often than other reflex ovulators have comparatively more unsuccessful mating periods.

The length of pregnancy in the big cats varies from species to species, from around 50 days for the bobcat to around 110 for the lioness. The number of young produced also varies from two to six. Cats of the genus *felis* generally produce more cubs in each litter than the females of the *panthera*.

The young are usually born blind and cannot walk for the first few days or weeks.

Left: A young cheetah photographed in Samburu in Kenya. Like all big cats it was born blind at least 95 days after conception. At first it would have been unable to walk, very delicate and prone to rickets and fragile bones. The male cheetah takes an active part in rearing the young. It helps to feed them by chewing down their food into small lumps which the young cheetah can digest more easily. At birth the cheetah has a thick mane which extends from head to tail. Only the paws and flanks are exposed and these show the typical markings of the adult. The mane is soon lost and the body is seen to be covered with closely spaced black spots on a tawny background. The spots merge into black rings on the tail.

Below: These little bundles of fur will soon grow up to be magnificent members of their species – the Chinese leopard. Our knowledge of the mating habits and rearing of the leopard is not fully developed because the courtship takes place in the denseness of the forests in which they live. Mating is, in all likelihood, a scratching, spitting match and when the young are born (probably three or four in each litter) they are carefully reared by the mother who brings them up to be as suspicious and wary as she is. The father takes no part in bringing up the young leopards – the female leaves him as soon as mating is complete and gives birth around 100 days later.

Below right: This five-week-old cheetah cub clearly shows the extent of the mane with which it is born. As it matures the coat takes on the richer colour that is typical of the breed. Also clearly seen in this shot is the black marking that runs from each side of the mouth up to the eye. If they are caught young enough, or bred in captivity, the cheetah can be well domesticated and makes an affectionate, but expensive, playmate. But its hunting instinct will always be present and it can revert at any time.

Gestation periods, the condition of the cubs, the number of cubs in each litter and other facts about big cats and their young vary from species to species – indeed from animal to animal. Just as no two human mothers will have identical pregnancies and look after their young in exactly the same way, so too, no two female lionesses or cheetahs or leopards will follow exactly the same behaviour pattern during and after gestation.

Pumas, leopards and jaguars have no fixed breeding seasons. They breed all the year round and the period of gestation varies from 90–93 days for the puma, 90–105 for the leopard and around 100 days for the jaguar. The usual size of the leopard litter seems to be two cubs but infant mortality is high and usually only one survives. The young are spotted at birth, but these spots tend to be greyer than the adult's. An interesting variation in the behaviour of the lioness and the leopard mother is that the lion cubs follow their mother around even when hunting. If they did not they would get no food from most small kills. The leopard cubs, however, seem to be more independent.

They are less likely to be with their mothers who leave the cubs behind when they hunt, fetching them to the hidden prey after a successful forage.

Young lionesses may stay within the mother's pride, but young male lions will be excluded by the mature males when they are about eighteen months old. Young leopards stay with their mothers until they are sub-adult. Then, the mother has taught them all the wiles and skills necessary to survive and the young go off to fend for themselves in their own territories.

Female pumas can have as many as four cubs in their litters. The young have spotted fur and ringed tails. They are weaned at around three months and stay with their parents for about two years by which time they will have lost their infant markings.

The breeding season of the tiger varies from area to area. In India, they breed all the year round, in Malaya mating takes place any time from November to March, but in Manchuria the tigers seem to breed only in December. Like all cats, young tigers are born blind. Their eyes open at around fourteen days and they are weaned at six weeks. By the age of seven months they are able to hunt on their own, although they normally stay with their mother until they are around two.

Cheetahs tend to have larger litters, anything up to six – although the average is about three. They are covered with a sort of cape which covers most of their bodies at first. The cubs are born and kept hidden in a thicket or under a bush and are moved around every day so that the litter escapes the attention of other predators. The mother has to leave the litter when she hunts, suckling them when she returns and, when they are weaned, regurgitating food for them. The litter leaves the protection of thick undergrowth and begins to follow the mother around at about four weeks old. Perhaps about fifty percent will survive and those that do develop rapidly achieve full size at around eighteen months. Then the family breaks up sometimes quite suddenly – one day they are with the mother, the next they are on their own.

Left: Lion cubs are fully dependent on milk for the first three months of life and the mother will cease to lactate about six to eight months after giving birth. During the intervening period the cubs are gradually weaned, obtaining an increasing proportion of their food from kills made by the adults of the pride. Nipple competition is fierce but because it is quite common for two or three females to have given birth at around the same time, the cubs can get milk from lionesses other than their mothers as communal suckling is quite common. As well as being a source of food and protection for the cub, the adults also offer shade from the relentless heat of the sun and small cubs can often be seen resting in the shadow cast by the adult members of the pride into which they have been born.

Left: The lioness gives birth to anything between one and six cubs, two to four being the norm. She normally goes off into a thicket to have them and keeps them hidden there for about six weeks. When she carries them around she lifts them in her mouth carrying them by the shoulders. The cubs are completely helpless at birth, so the lioness will move them around at intervals to escape the attention of predators such as leopards and hyaenas which will have no hesitation in killing any defenceless cubs they come across. Like the adult lions, the cubs spend most of their days sleeping. Unfortunately, cub mortality is high – some prides lose almost all the cubs that are born, others manage to ensure that the majority are brought into adulthood. Some deaths are accidental, due to careless mothering, some are due to disease and some cubs will be lost to predators or killed during their early hunting days. Some die of starvation.

Right: The two cheetah cubs seen here with their mother are obviously well on the road to a successful adulthood – although there is about a 50% mortality rate during the first year of life. The cubs weigh about 10 oz (75 g) at birth but when they are mature adults their weight can exceed 100 lb (45 kg).

Right: Bobcat kittens may be born at any time of the year, but the usual time is in late February and March. It has been known for a female bobcat to produce two litters in one year, but this is most unusual. Gestation takes between 50 and 60 days and the young are blind for their first week. The mother gives birth in her den, in caves, under logs or occasionally under a farmyard barn. Two kittens are normal for each litter and the mother will defend them vigorously, especially from the father who is kept well away until the kittens are weaned. At this stage, the father will help collect food for the family. When fully grown, the kittens will be around 3 ft (1 m) long and will weigh, on average, 20 lb (9 kg).

Left: This three-month-old baby jaguar already displays the markings of the adult – the yellowish ground colour of the coat becoming paler underneath and the arrangement of the spots, four or five around a central spot. Note that the spots are more tightly packed on the head and legs. Adult jaguars breed at all times of the year and gestation lasts about 100 days. Normally two to four cubs are born in each litter. Because jaguars are difficult to find in their forest haunts, their coats blending so well with the background, much less is known about them than about other cats.

Above right: The mother leopard and her cubs merge well with the colouring of their forest lair. There does not appear to be a breeding season for leopards – whenever a female is in oestrus mating takes place repeatedly for a few days and the gestation period is about three months. The mother leaves her young to hunt and when she has made a successful kill returns to the lair and takes her cubs back to where she has hidden the prey. The young start to hunt on a trial and error basis, beginning with small animals and birds but remain fairly dependent on the mother who shares larger prey with her offspring until they are well able to fend for themselves.

Right: An Asiatic lioness (*Panthera leo persica*) is seen coming out of its hide in obvious attacking mood. The Asiatic lions are an increasingly rare breed and most, if not all of them, live in the Gir forest in India. Here they can live in comparative safety from man and can breed and bring their young up in their natural environment as the species is now protected by law. A census taken in 1968 puts their numbers at around 170. As with all big cats, the lioness is extremely protective of her cubs and will not hesitate to strike out to defend them.

Below left: The black panther, which is a melanistic leopard (*Panthera pardus*) shares the same breeding characteristics as the normally coloured leopard. It is found in Asia and in the islands of Indonesia. Facial expression plays an important part in communication. Both the panther and the Asiatic Golden Cat (**above left**) have a wide variety of facial signals which are often directed at intruders. By opening their mouths and drawing back their lips they make their formidable teeth visible to adversaries. This is reinforced by snarls and hisses making it clear to an intruder that it advances at its own risk. Female cats are at their most dangerous when protecting their young from possible danger.

Right: Serval cats usually mate in the spring and produce young after about 70 days. They generally have their young hidden in their dens in the grasses of the savannah. One advantage that the serval cat has over other big cats is that it is more adaptable to environment. It feeds upon reptiles and small antelopes and is adept at catching birds, being well able to climb into bushes and ravage any nestlings and fledglings it may find.

Big Cats and men

Lions and tigers used to be the favourite pets of kings and nobles. It was a way of showing off how powerful they were. Nero is said to have shared his table with a tigress called Phoebe who was sometimes given humans who had incurred the emperor's wrath.

We still refer to lions as the 'king of the jungle': we talk about being 'as sharp eyed as a lynx' or moving 'with the speed of a cheetah': we think of the tiger as 'burning bright, through the jungle in the night'.

Big cats have captivated the imaginations of many men,

have been used as the symbols of power and of sovereignty and in many parts of the world have been wiped out as a supposed threat to man, his crops and his domestic animals.

The ancient Romans used to put gladiators in the ring with lions and sit back and watch the ensuing fight, shouting for blood and delighting in the eventual bloodbath. Lions were also used to draw the chariots of emperors entering the city in triumph.

The lion became the symbol of the city state of Venice and statues of it there still show the lion lying with its paw on top of a book. Local legend claims that when the book was open the city was at war, when it was closed it was at peace.

Lions have been used in the fables of Leonardo and of Aesop. As a symbol of courage it was adopted by Richard I of England – Richard *Coeur de Lion*. It can be seen on the coat of arms of the British monarchy, and on the flag of Scotland – the lion rampant. As it appears on the coats of arms of many English towns and cities, the lion can be seen on the hallmarks of much of the silver sold in British jewellers and antique shops.

Naturally, as the lion is indigenous to Africa, there are a great many local legends concerning the king of beasts. One Lybian one is similar to an old Roman belief that lions would not attack a woman. But how many women there were who could give testimony to this belief is a question of some speculation. The Somalis believed that the lion was sent by God to punish them. First, he thought he would send the roar which would be enough to frighten the troublesome natives, but it wasn't, so he sent the lion itself.

The Indians of Guyana tell an interesting story about the jaguar. It seems that one jaguar followed a herd of peccaries for some time feeding off those that became separated from the herd. This went on for some time until the peccaries turned on the jaguar and chased it up a tree. They surrounded the tree and formed a screaming mob around it. The petrified jaguar lowered its tail which one peccary grabbed and pulled. The jaguar tumbled from the tree to be ripped apart by the herd.

The tiger is, to the islanders of Sumatra, the reincarnation of some fellow islander and as such is held in high regard. Not quite as high, though, as the Chinese of the Amur river who make offerings wherever they find a tiger's footprint. Some part of the tigers' bodies are held to be beneficial for certain ailments – the liver, for example, is thought to bring relief to those suffering from blood diseases.

But no matter how feared or worshipped the big cats are, the sad fact is that man has almost hunted many of them off the face of the earth. This is not a new problem. The demand for lions for

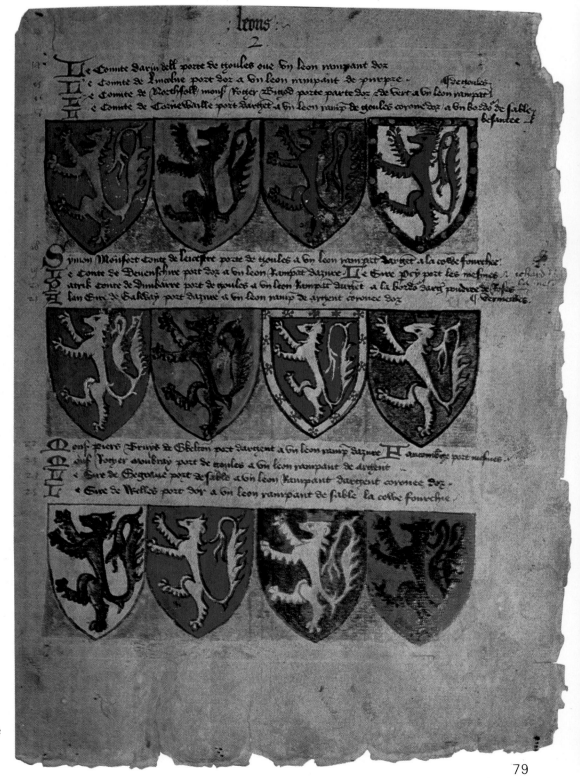

Left: The English Royal Standard shows on the right a unicorn and on the left a lion rampant. Lions have long played a part in heraldry – here the lion is used to symbolize the power and strength of the monarch. The motto 'dieu et mon droit' means 'God and my right hand' and has been the motto of the British royal family for many centuries.
Right: The Jenyns Book of Arms, made *c.*1410 and originally owned by Margaret of Anjou, shows the various coats of arms of the major families of the time. This page clearly shows how popular lions were among heraldic symbols.

the Roman circuses was so great that the lions of North Africa were dreadfully overhunted.

Just as the cats themselves are hunters, so too, is man. He started off by surviving in the cruel environment of prehistoric times, pitting his wits against other predators and gaining mastery over them by gradually using his developing intelligence. The hunting instinct is still strong in man. But in choosing the big cats as his adversaries, often shooting at them from the safety of the back of an elephant, man chose a range of species that posed little threat to himself. True, there are occasions when the big cats turn maneater, but, as we have already said, such animals are usually old and infirm or have in some way become unable to hunt their normal prey. True, big cats have, in some areas, taken to feeding off animal livestock, but only in areas where their natural environment has been threatened by the advance of agriculture and the big cats' natural prey has been forced back or, indeed, hunted by man. True, there have been reports of men and women being savaged by big cats, but generally only if the cat feels itself threatened in some way. So why have men taken to hunt them? For three main reasons. Firstly, because the cats pose some threat, real or imaginary, to local natives and farmers. Secondly, for sport, but thankfully 'big game hunting' is now almost a thing of the past. When hunters go to shoot big cats nowadays, it is cameras rather than guns that they aim. And lastly, for vanity. A fur coat has been a status symbol for generations. But simulated furs are now of such quality and the pro 'big cat lobby' is now so vociferous, that the trading in furs is not nearly so great as it was and modern science has given us methods of producing simulated furs that are almost impossible to tell apart from genuine fur coats.

It must be remembered that the cats themselves are beneficial to man because of the part that they play in maintaining the ecological balance of an area, and if this delicate balance is tampered with too dramatically – who knows what the consequences would be?

Der Tiger.   DE TIJGER.   THE TIGER.

Above: Will he manage to pull the trigger in time? For his sake one must hope so, but for the sake of the tiger –? Tiger hunting was a popular sport among the maharajas of India and European colonists and hunters of the nineteenth and early twentieth centuries. Tiger skin rugs and mounted heads adorned the floors and walls of smart houses and clubs in many European capitals. But then it was realized that the tiger had been overhunted and was in danger of extinction, so laws have been passed in many countries where the tiger is still found naturally, banning anyone from hunting them. It is to be hoped that this has not come too late and that the tiger will not die out completely as a wild animal.

Right: A newspaper cover of the 1890s shows the coverage that big-game hunting was given in the Press of the day. Many of the hunters were European aristocrats, such as the Duke of Orleans shown here, who organized safaris to India and Africa and carried their trophies back to Europe with them to decorate the floors and walls of their mansions.

THE GRAPHIC

AN ILLUSTRATED WEEKLY NEWSPAPER

No. 1,018.—Vol. XXXIX.
Registered as a Newspaper

SATURDAY, JUNE 1, 1889

THIRTY-TWO PAGES
AND EXTRA SUPPLEMENT

PRICE SIXPENCE
By Post 6½*d.*

"AT CLOSE QUARTERS"

AN INCIDENT OF THE DUC D'ORLEANS' RECENT HUNTING TOUR IN INDIA

Chas. E. Fripp.

Left: These two water-colours are based on sketches by Captain Robert Baden-Powell, better known as founder of the Boy Scouts than as an artist. They show a white hunter (**top**) facing a lion near the Zambesi. The hunters would trek around after the herds of antelope and buffalo knowing that the lions would not be far away. The Boer (**below**) is hunting a leopard, not for sport, but because the cat has been attacking his flocks.

Above: Even when dead, the heads of the cats being displayed for sale in Nairobi still maintain a ferocious anger.

Above: Lion cubs which have been separated from their pride and which are unable to look after themselves in the wild have been reared successfully by humans. A baby's bottle and reinforced teat can take the place of a mother's nipple. It is interesting to note the way in which this young cub is using its front paws to grasp the bottle. One of the best descriptions of rearing a young cub can be found in Joy Adamson's book *Born Free*. In it she describes how she 'adopted' a young cub and successfully reared it to adulthood, returning it to the wild to fend for itself when the time was right. A strong bond was built up between cub and surrogate mother which lasted even after the lion was living free in the savannah of Kenya.

Left: This cub was successfully raised in captivity in Rapid City, South Dakota, as an experiment. Even when quite large, the cub still obviously enjoyed being rubbed down after a bath!

Right: Being intelligent creatures, tigers can be trained to perform various tricks and stunts that have delighted circus audiences for hundreds of years. But no matter how well cared for the animals are, there is something pathetic about the sight of a great beast that should be living naturally and free rearing up on its hind legs and pawing at the air, responding to the crack of a whip merely for the entertainment of an audience. Tigers are apparently the most difficult of all the big cats to train for performance. Lions are much more easily trained, perhaps because they are sociable cats and are used to working within the framework of a group, even with a human in charge.

Despite the bans on hunting big cats in many parts of the world, there is still an extensive trade in the skins and heads of these animals. The picture (**above**) shows the dealings in tiger skins in Srinagar in Nepal. The pelts will be cured and exported to furriers in the West where they are made into fur coats worn by expensively-dressed women in the fashionable streets of the world. Desmond Morris, the zoologist and sociologist considers that the women who wear them are 'performing the last act in a primitive triumph, in which the remnants of the vanquished are displayed as adornments on the bodies of tribal victors'.

The trade in skins is also carried on in South America as the picture (**left**) demonstrates. Here we can see jaguar skins being packed for export. But none of this is now necessary. Modern science has produced methods of simulating these furs to such a degree that it is almost impossible to tell which is the real skin and which is man-made. The model (**far left**) is wearing an artificial lynx fur coat. Probably only the lynx can tell the difference.

Zoos and game parks

No one knows for sure which civilization first kept wild animals. There is evidence that Queen Hatshepsut of Egypt kept leopards in her menagerie several thousand years ago. The Indian princes kept stables of cheetahs which they used when hunting. The Emperor Nero had a pet tigress and one of the gifts that Charlemagne received from the Caliph of Baghdad (after dropping several broad hints) was a splendid lion.

Today many major cities of the world boast zoological gardens among their tourist attractions – places where the public can come and gaze (and occasionally be gazed at by the animals themselves) at animals which they would not otherwise be able to see. From London to St Louis, Sydney to Antwerp a vast amount of money has been spent in importing wild animals and building 'houses' for them.

The evolution of the public zoo as we know it today began in France during the reign of Louis XIV. Louis made a special hobby of his menageries which at the time tended to be planned in a rather careless fashion. Aviaries would be sited well away from the lion-houses which were probably some distance from the bear pits. When Louis was involved in the planning of his splendid palace at Versailles he decided to concentrate all his animals together in a 'menagerie du Parc' with all the cages and enclosures close together. This eventually fell into disrepair and was ransacked by a hostile mob during the French Revolution. They were wise enough not to tamper with the lions and rhinoceros and a few other fearsome beasts, but who, the director of the gardens had to ask himself, was going to look after them? Eventually they were sent to the *Jardin des Plantes*, after a great deal of opposition from its director, Bernardin de Sainte-Pierre. However, the conservative scientists who used the jardin for serious botanical study did welcome the animals that began to arrive from all over France, but they insisted that the zoo should not become a peepshow and that the animals should be treated with some respect.

The zoo in Paris was such a success that more were opened up in Europe over the next century. In London, a group of men under the leadership of Sir Stamford Raffles, Sir Humphrey Davy and Sir Joseph Banks (who accompanied Captain Cook on his first voyage of discovery) held a meeting to form themselves into a Zoological Society the aim of which was to introduce . . . 'new and curious objects of the Animal Kingdom'. They expected opposition and they got it! But eventually they were permitted by the Commissioners of Woods and Forests to put cages up in five acres of Regent's Park in central London. The king, who was nominal owner of the park, obviously approved for when he died he bequeathed half the contents of his private royal menagerie at Windsor to the Zoological Society.

Soon imitations were springing up everywhere on the Continent as well as Britain. Originally, the wild animals were

Above: A Siberian Tiger photographed in its zoo cage. Fortunately many zoos now have large compounds where the big cats are given much more space and such sights as this are less common than they were in earlier zoos.

Far left: Singh, one of the popular attractions in the lion house at London Zoo in Regents Park. The idea of a zoo in London was first suggested by Sir Stamford Raffles, the founder of Singapore in 1826 but his idea was met with ridicule. 'We do not know how the inhabitants of Regent's Park will like the lions, leopards and linxes so near their neighbourhood', wrote an anonymous contributor to the *Literary Gazette*. But eventually five acres of the park were leased from the crown and the zoo was so popular that this had to be extended.

kept in well-barred cages. The sight of proud lions and tigers pacing back and forth in their narrow cages is not particularly pleasant. Things changed when Carl Hagenbeck decided to build a zoo that would be different from any other in the world. He bought land at Stellingen in Germany. He wished to exhibit the animals 'not as captives, confined within narrow spaces but as free to wander from place to place within as large limits as possible'. His park was opened in 1907 and was an

immediate success. Wide enclosures surrounded by moats were constructed to resemble the natural habitats of the animals themselves. The big cats were 'housed' in a 'Carnivore Glen' with rooms at the back where the animals retreated at night. Zoos everywhere began to copy Hagenbeck's methods and his influence is still seen today.

Many of the zoos have had a great deal of success in breeding the big cats. At Whipsnade, in England, where no attempt has been made to build artificial environments for the big cats, the third generation of zoo-bred cheetahs can be seen basking in the rolling parkland of rural England.

At Howletts Zoo Park in Kent, a private zoo owned by John Aspinall the largest breeding colony of Indian and Siberian tigers in the world has been established. Aspinall has also built up a remarkable bond of affection between himself and the tigers. He bought his first one for £200 in 1958 and today, more than 20 years later, more than 40 of her descendents are alive and well in various parts of the world (although she was killed

Below: A mother cheetah and her cubs at Whipsnade Zoo in England, where cheetahs have now been bred for three generations. Cheetahs obviously adapt well to life away from their natural environment and, if they are caught young enough, or born in captivity, they are quite easy to train and make affectionate playmates; although, like all wild animals, they can revert to their natural instincts quite easily.

by her mate when she was thirteen).

Obviously, no matter how wide a space a cat has in captivity, it is unable to obtain its food by hunting. As meat eaters they are fed meat regularly, but to obviate the natural health dangers of a predatory life, additives are given to prevent infections and malformations and to ensure healthy development of the young.

Zoos have brought wild animals to us and have ensured that some species that may be in danger of extinction are now safely re-established, albeit out of their own environment. But how much better are the wildlife parks that have been established throughout the world. In America, India and Africa vast areas have been set aside where the wild animals can live protected from man the hunter.

A great deal of knowledge of lions, cheetahs and leopards has come from the Serengeti in Africa. In an area of about 5,000 sq. miles (8,000 sq. km) made up of woodland, undulating hills and grass, the big cats can live as naturally as nature intended –

free to roam the savannah lands, to hunt for their food, to rear their young so that future generations of man can look at them and appreciate the awesome beauty of the big cats.

But if the big cats are to survive in their natural surroundings, the human population of the areas where the cats are found has to be re-educated to a certain extent. In 1979, five rare tigers were spotted near a settlement in North India. The Indian Government wanted to resettle the villagers, but they tried to insist that they remained in their houses and that the government hunted and killed the threatened tigers!

Below: It is fortunate that clouded leopards have been successfully kept in captivity, otherwise most of us would never have the chance of seeing these beautiful animals.
Overleaf: The Marquis of Bath has had a great deal of success with the wildlife park that he has built up in the grounds of his stately home at Longleat in Wiltshire, England. Motorists who drive through the park have a rare chance to see prides of lions lazing around in the English countryside.

Right: A strong warning is given to visitors to the Smith-Lion County Safariland park in California.
Below: Anyone visiting the park is strongly advised to stay in their car while driving through the park. Despite warnings, a few misguided souls have ventured from their cars to feed the lions!
Far right: John Aspinall has developed a unique relationship with the tigers at his Howletts Zoo Park in Kent. Here he relaxes with an adult male and female and two cubs.

INDEX

Acknowledgements
The publishers would like to thank the following individuals and organizations for their kind permission to reproduce the photographs in this book:

G. V. Adkin Title page, endpapers, 30-31, 62-63 below, 66 above, 66-67 below, 67 above; Ardea, London 47, 55 above, 87 above, (McDougal Tiger Tops) 44-45, 52-53, (P. Morris) 83; Beth Bergman 33 above; Bruce Coleman Incorporated 76 below, (John S. Flannery) 74 below, (G. D. Plage) 42 above, (Diana and Rick Sullivan) 18, 26 below; Bruce Coleman Ltd. (R. I. M. Campbell) 56-57, (Mary Grant) 46 above, 54, 75 above, (Peter Jackson) 51 below, (P. Kahl) introduction, (Gordon Langsbury) contents, (Leonard lee Rue III) 74 above, (Norman Myers) 15, 27, 73 above, (Dieter and Mary Plage) 47 below, (Goetz D. Plage) ½ title, 72, (Hans Reinhard) 58-59, 64-65, (Dick Robinson) 20-21, 33 below, (George B. Schaller) 55 below, (Simon Trevor) 34-35, (Joe van Wormer) 14; Gerald Cubitt 9 above, 12-13 below, 60-61, 68-69, 77; The Daily Telegraph Colour Library 86; Mary Evans Picture Library 80; Grant Heilman 29; Howletts Zoo Park and Port Lympne Wildlife Park (Clive Boursnell) 95 above and below; Alan Hutchison Library 12 below; Jacana (L. Chana) 60 left, (Jean-Philippe Varin) 48-49, (Varin Visage) 19 above, (Ziesler) 19 below; The Mansell Collection Ltd. 81, 82 above, 82 below; Jean Morris 63 above; Marion and Tony Morrison 87 below; Natural Science Photos (J. Hobday) 50; Oxford Scientific Films (J. A. L. Cooke) 8, (Leonard lee Rue III) 10, 11, (Stouffer Productions) 9 below; Oxford Scientific Films/Animals, Animals (Fran Allan) 12 above left, 62 above, (M. Austerman) 24 above, 28, 43, (Tom Brakefield) 41, (Patricia Caulfield) 84 above, (Jerry Cooke) 89, (Tex Fuller) 36-37 below, (Leonard lee Rue III) 40, (Z. Leszczynski) 51 above, (S. D. Mag) 94 below, (Charles Palek) 84 below, (Ranjitsinh) 23, (Bradley Smith) 94 above, (Stouffer Enterprises Inc.) 26 above, (Mark Stouffer) 32, 38-39, (Stouffer Productions Ltd.) 36 above, (Ernest Wilkinson) 42-43 below; Picturepoint, London 38 inset above, 73 below, 78, 79, 92-93; Mandal Ranjit 75 below; Spectrum Colour Library 25, 71; Shin Yoshino 16-17, 22, 24 below, 76 above, 91; Zefa (F. Walther) 85; The Zoological Society of London 70, 88, 90.

Picture Research: Tessa Politzer